ADULTING

MADELAINE JONES

First Published in December 2021

Published and typeset by Madelaine Jones
Cover illustration by Harry Thory (@hptx)

www.madelainejones.co.uk
@MadelaineJonesCreative

ISBN 978-1-7398600-0-4

CONTENTS

for andrea

DRUNK THOUGHTS

it is the golden hour
when the hangover
is just an imaginary pet
coiled in your lap
not yet materialised

road stumblers and kebab-hunters
slur in your eyes
with drift and noise and vodka mixers
as the driver releases his hold
head hooking onto the swerve
at the centre of a gyroscope
pickled suspended and numb

you chew on fresh plans
from who knows where
and what or even
who you are anymore
but now they are your pillow

and after the morning after
they'll be the thing that clings
that you can't aspirin away
the undoable scrt-scrt
scratching in your head

OFFICE WORKER

i am there but not there
filling 9 hours with a game of
isn't this a thoughtfully placed button
click scroll click
why yes that was a remarkably long pee
does anyone want a cup of tea?
popping out to the shops
for a prawn sandwich prosecco hummus basil gochujang
picture frames birthday cards witch hazel charity shop bargains
back for the obligatory half-hour email responses
and the same yes my weekend was fine how was yours
because they balked that time i told them
i spent christmas morning in hospital
and it was coming out both ends

4 DAYS

i haven't said anything new in 4 days

i
got a new job
decided to buy a house
told a friend i might end us
scored a date on the internet
with a girl with a nose ring
and all you know is
what you asked about

- why i bought brown basmati instead of white

- how sore my knees are after pilates

- have the cats been fed yet this evening

- did i pick up a lemon from waitrose on my way home

LEVEL 3 AND RISING

level 3 and rising
in two minutes from human to worker
grey knees matching grey eyes
matching grey shadows
matching grey oh why is everything so fucking grey building

i don't think we were made
to be embalmed alive in cubicles
i've no idea if we all feel the same
or if the woman to my left
bleeds spreadsheets and bullshit
when she gets a papercut

but one thing is certain
we all know the convoluted rules
of her new year detox diet
inside out

get me out of this fucking lift
i'd rather stay at the bottom

ONE RING

it’s weighing round his neck
he needs to shit or get off the pot
and put it on already

REFLECT

sometimes
everything
the moon
catching gold
shredding silver
high baby god
observer on a dancing tapestry

and sometimes
nothing
dry lake
cracked bed
no ebb no flow
no mirror
absorbing
existing
eating
huh

STALE

crossed fingers
don't stop the bread
from going stale

i've read on reddit
you can pop it in the microwave
with a sexy little bowl of water
30 seconds at 1000W

next thing you know
it's springy and hot
and the steam makes it soft
fresh for a bit

not forever
perhaps i'll just nibble
pick at the crusts
waiting for the mould to take hold
so i can swipe right
on a new loaf

POLY

i.
you're through the door
grinning at a job well done
face split like kiwifruit
eyelash tar smeared on your cheek

my stomach flicks
a hiccup of twinge
when i see the black
a buccal brand

and then back in the room
scooping stories from their skins
with your arms like a sling
and me filling the middle

then the part i love most
when you tell me how much you missed me

ii.
it used to be an appetiser
when your mouth tasted of hers
a whetstone to spark my tongue against
flash-in-the-pan hot

now it is straining against my underwire
and vacuum-sealing my insides
it isn't even that you smell of her
you smell of the best version of you
the one normally reserved for job interviews

the musk reminds me that
mine never meant mine entirely

iii.
the older i get
the less my head
and my vagina
seem to agree

ROUTINE

i want to swipe left on mornings
they taste like struggle
ungluing lids and unsticking joints
with a half-empty tub of E45

SHOES

sandals socks bare boots
i measure the days by shoes
flicking past my
feet calendar toes
turn the page and
garden home bath funeral

tongues soles flapping
thirsty for superglue
something that sticks
and does not keep
moving and breaking and
wearing down

roulette again
outside inside
black red straight street
even pair odd socks
fingers crossed
still coming up zero

GRAPEFRUIT

some days i feel like
a grapefruit with the pith missing
uncushioned in an empty skin
flesh rolling from palm to palm
offered up and passed on
and turned down for
an apple or a banana
something smooth or expected
perfect slutty fruit
that everyone wants
in their mouths

i want to roll off the counter
screaming in protest
dimpled with cellulite
speckled and difficult
but my fat buttocks
would hit the ground
too softly for catharsis

BED

i.

sometimes
my head is in moscow
and my body is in california
shivering awake in odd timezones
transliterating under the covers

ii.

sometimes
i turn and face
the other way
when i'm sleeping
but your breath on my neck
means i can't pretend
you're not there

DO YOU CALL HER BABYGIRL?

she is an insoluble concept
i watch you swallow whole
dribble everywhere
until the floor is slippy
and your nape is
soaked in her

crying in your lap
when we get back
a dry prune
left in the bag for weeksmonthsyears
begging you to
put me in your mouth
and tell me how sweet i am

ANAESTHETIC

this is the part
where i tell you
to fuck off
if you don't like it

chain-vaper
binge-drinker
kalms-popper
i anaesthetise myself
when i've had enough

that doesn't make me broken
who wouldn't go insane
without a steam valve
in this madhouse
where the world snaps black necks like twigs
and pussy-grabbers govern wombs

BUDDING

it has roots
and soon it will grow
ten metres tall
twenty years wide
yellow lax and happy
flower child
from seed to tower
the prettiest yet

***

on the sofa
empty pot damp soil
i wonder if it was the cat
or manslaughter
or perhaps i just
imagined it
in the first place

i spot its twin
smug bastard
in the corner
drooping but alive
take the scissors
hack at the leaves
watch it shed
death confetti in the mirror
unable to do anything
good or bad
or at all

SHAME

most of the time
i forget it's there
until it's not
like when you don't realise you're ill
until you wake up and your nose
isn't blocked anymore

BEDBOUND

acid sun striking flesh
and i'm writhing
like rotisserie meat
on a duvet garnish

today is escaping my fingertips
i can't reach or run after it
nothing of me can run
except the sweat from my head neck chest stomach
thigh knees crack legs feet liquid heat
dripping-down-soaked into the mattress
pooled in my belly button
and in there
i save my oasis
dry as mouthfuls of sand
and soaked at the same time

TRADE

i know she has more xp
but if you keep grinding
i'll evolve without a stone
i promise

please don't trade
me in just yet
please

PLACEBO

today i bought a crystal
an amethyst pendant
on a thin silver chain
with a plaque explaining
how it would change my life
this little purple bolt
ripping through the seams
of anything negative

it's bollocks of course
but it's a talisman
even adults need bedtime stories
it's a rock i can hold onto
a little violet nugget
that does absolutely nothing
but exist in reality
(unlike any of us)

FATIGUE

i never realised how strong
the craving to stop could get
to just lie down and give in

GRANDFATHER

you text me from downstairs
to tell me your grandad has died
by the time i wake up
you're gone
full speed ahead
to wembley or wimbledon
wherever it is

when you come back
i look for the cogs
but nothing
you're still ticking
perfect time

just a small nod to the fact
he'll never get to try
the cantal you birthed

milk rennet curds
press brine
aging
love

and then blank
as you always are
and it makes me feel special
that sometimes when we fight
you have to fight back tears

SPOONS

clammy skin pressed
like folded prawns
sweating all night
just to wrap my fingers
in your chest hair
while you snore

then rumbling
the salt of your back
sliding you free
armpits flared

cool air hitting my bare chest
waking up to roll over
and hug too tightly
until you slip out
once every couple of hours
a dance of together-apart
hot-cold wet-dry
you-me

you never remember our dream tango
in the morning when the alarm meows
but your arms each night
sweeping love radar
find me and map me

SPUDS

heads sprouting
you mumble
that sometimes you wonder
if we are both sad
then what is the point

and the question   hangs

and i remember
that even when
you say nothing
you are in there
under there
scared with me
restless roots
tangled in dirt

between us
we have the arms
to pull this spud
out of the ground
and dust it down
to gold

grab your shovel partner
there's shit to get through

ADULTING

16 17 18
they warned us all about
contraception writing a cv
the bills and the taxes
mortgage kids car
counting beans and
dishing out dust
with a salad
on a side plate

but no hint about
how it feels
not quite knowing
if something fits
or we just don't want
to imagine it doesn't
gripping so hard
our fingers turn purplewhite

DREAMS

sleeping in pieces
scrawled on the sheets
in crayola peach
closed-lid animations
disjointed flashes of yesterday
or tomorrow
or that weird moment
with you and maybe perhaps
go on you can do it
if you try hard enough
but then mum tells you
not today because
the spanakopita ate the cat
no you can't

and the frame shifts
and our house is not our house
and your face is not your face
and i am not me any more
.... (but i sort of still am)
zzz
..
z
.

and none of it makes sense
but if i'm honest
sometimes that happens
even when i'm awake
at midday on a friday
or in the pub
or on the bus home
breathing in and sneezing out
other futures
where this doesn't hurt
until you hold my hand
and help pull me back

EGGS AND A CUPPA

nowadays sexy is
scrambled eggs
waiting with a cuppa
and a deep kiss
when you remember to
open your lips

the last time i tried to
feel like new
my hips spilled over my lingerie
like excess playdough
peeled free for
one strike and out
zonko

so breakfast kisses
a once-a-week fumble
two if i'm lucky

i'm settling in at last
it's alright actually
could be worse

BECOMING MY MOTHER

give me a cheeky fag
a weak glass of robinson's
fruit and barley
and a good piece of gossip
and it's there
in the way we both shout
go on my son at the telly
or cry with laughter
flashing a tit at each other
through the kitchen window

PIECES

in japan
they piece things back together
when they crack
fill the veins with gold
and celebrate the scars
because it means you were there
you survived and you grew

here we collect the pieces
frame the last attempt
like a roadmap
mark out the potholes
the roundabouts
we got stuck on

and upgrade
throw a new one
into the kiln
then wait
for the warmth
to seal its shape

CHOUX

food is how we translate
words within layers of filo
envelopes of mouth-hug
flaking in our fingers

cold hands warm heart
you roll with a half-empty wine bottle
stretching to flat
teasing until you
strip two strands
from the ribbon of pale dough

laughter like choux
bite and it gushes
sugar and cream
puffed with pride
piping bag spent
full and happy

TIME

when you're walking
in the right direction
the only thing
left to
add is
tick
tock
tick
tock
tick
tock
tick
tock
tick
tock
tick
tock
tick
-
.

Printed in Great Britain
by Amazon

71943680R00021